I0821014

THE PRAYER MAP® for Gutsy Girls

BARBOUR
PUBLISHING

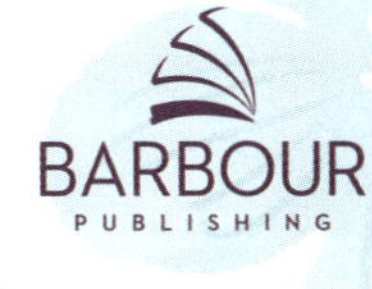

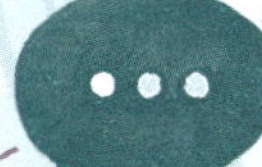

Print ISBN 979-8-89151-036-4

Published by Barbour Publishing, Inc., 1810 Barbour Drive, Uhrichsville, Ohio 44683, www.barbourbooks.com

Our mission is to inspire the world with the life-changing message of the Bible.

Printed in China.

This engaging and creative tool will help guide you into powerful prayer, as each colorful page prompts you to create your very own prayer map—to write specific thoughts, ideas, and lists—which you can follow (from start to finish!) as you talk to God. (Be sure to record the date on each one of your prayer maps so you can look back over time and see how God has continued to work in your life!)

The Prayer Map for Gutsy Girls will not only help you find the courage to pray big, bold prayers. . .it will also help you build a healthy spiritual habit of continual prayer for life!

Can it be that God will actually move into our neighborhood? Why, the cosmos itself isn't large enough to give you breathing room, let alone this Temple I've built. Even so, I'm bold to ask: Pay attention to these my prayers, both intercessory and personal, O God, my God. Listen to my prayers, energetic and devout, that I'm setting before you right now.

1 Kings 8:27–28 MSG

DATE:

Dear Heavenly Father,

My gutsy prayer for today is. . .

I need You to. . .

With You by my side, I am unafraid because. . .

I believe You are the doer of the impossible because. . .

I know You will. . .

Please give me the strength and courage I need today.

THANK YOU, FATHER, FOR HEARING MY PRAYERS!

Amen.

Light, space, zest—that's God! So, with him on my side I'm fearless, afraid of no one and nothing.

Psalm 27:1 MSG

DATE:

Dear Heavenly Father,

My gutsy prayer for today is. . .

I need You to. . .

With You by my side, I am unafraid because. . .

I believe You are the doer of the impossible because. . .

I know You will. . .

Please give me the strength and courage I need today.

THANK YOU, FATHER, FOR HEARING MY PRAYERS!

amen.

"Your Father knows what you need before you ask Him."
MATTHEW 6:8 NLV

DATE:

Dear Heavenly Father,

My gutsy prayer for today is. . .

I need You to. . .

With You by my side, I am unafraid because. . .

I believe You are the doer of the impossible because. . .

I know You will. . .

Please give me the strength and courage I need today.

THANK YOU, FATHER, FOR HEARING MY PRAYERS!

Amen.

"Be strong and courageous. Don't tremble! Don't be afraid of them! The Lord *your God is the one who is going with you. He won't abandon you or leave you."*

Deuteronomy 31:6 GW

DATE:

Dear Heavenly Father,

My gutsy prayer for today is. . .

I need You to. . .

With You by my side, I am unafraid because. . .

I believe You are the doer of the impossible because. . .

I know You will. . .

Please give me the strength and courage I need today.

THANK YOU, FATHER, FOR HEARING MY PRAYERS!

Amen.

"The Lord is with us. Do not be afraid."

Numbers 14:9 NLV

DATE:

Dear Heavenly Father,

My gutsy prayer for today is. . .

I need You to. . .

With You by my side, I am unafraid because. . .

I believe You are the doer of the impossible because. . .

I know You will. . .

Please give me the strength and courage I need today.

THANK YOU, FATHER, FOR HEARING MY PRAYERS!

amen.

I have the strength to face all conditions by the power that Christ gives me.

PHILIPPIANS 4:13 GNT

DATE:

Dear Heavenly Father,

My gutsy prayer for today is. . .

I need You to. . .

With You by my side, I am unafraid because. . .

I believe You are the doer of the impossible because. . .

I know You will. . .

Please give me the strength and courage I need today.

THANK YOU, FATHER, FOR HEARING MY PRAYERS!

Amen.

"Don't panic. I'm with you. There's no need to fear for I'm your God. I'll give you strength. I'll help you. I'll hold you steady, keep a firm grip on you."

ISAIAH 41:10 MSG

DATE:

Dear Heavenly Father,

My gutsy prayer for today is. . .

I need You to. . .

With You by my side, I am unafraid because. . .

I believe You are the doer of the impossible because. . .

I know You will. . .

Please give me the strength and courage I need today.

THANK YOU, FATHER, FOR HEARING MY PRAYERS!

amen.

But those who trust in the Lord for help will find their strength renewed. They will rise on wings like eagles; they will run and not get weary; they will walk and not grow weak.

Isaiah 40:31 GNT

DATE:

Dear Heavenly Father,

My gutsy prayer for today is. . .

I need You to. . .

With You by my side, I am unafraid because. . .

I believe You are the doer of the impossible because. . .

I know You will. . .

Please give me the strength and courage I need today.

THANK YOU, FATHER, FOR HEARING MY PRAYERS!

Amen.

The LORD is my strong defender; he is the one who has saved me. He is my God, and I will praise him, my father's God, and I will sing about his greatness.

EXODUS 15:2 GNT

DATE:

Dear Heavenly Father,

My gutsy prayer for today is. . .

I need You to. . .

With You by my side, I am unafraid because. . .

I believe You are the doer of the impossible because. . .

I know You will. . .

Please give me the strength and courage I need today.

THANK YOU, FATHER, FOR HEARING MY PRAYERS!

Amen.

*"Search for the LORD and his strength.
Always seek his presence."*
1 CHRONICLES 16:11 GW

DATE:

Dear Heavenly Father,

My gutsy prayer for today is. . .

I need You to. . .

With You by my side, I am unafraid because. . .

For the Spirit that God has given us does not make us timid; instead, his Spirit fills us with power, love, and self-control.

2 TIMOTHY 1:7 GNT

DATE:

Dear Heavenly Father,

My gutsy prayer for today is. . .

I need You to. . .

With You by my side, I am unafraid because. . .

I believe You are the doer of the impossible because. . .

I know You will. . .

Please give me the strength and courage I need today.

THANK YOU, FATHER, FOR HEARING MY PRAYERS!

Amen.

"I have commanded you, 'Be strong and courageous! Don't tremble or be terrified, because the Lord *your God is with you wherever you go.' "*

Joshua 1:9 GW

DATE:

Dear Heavenly Father,

My gutsy prayer for today is. . .

I need You to. . .

With You by my side, I am unafraid because. . .

Keep your eyes open, hold tight to your convictions, give it all you've got, be resolute, and love without stopping.

1 Corinthians 16:13–14 MSG

DATE:

Dear Heavenly Father,

My gutsy prayer for today is. . .

I need You to. . .

With You by my side, I am unafraid because. . .

I believe You are the doer of the impossible because. . .

I know You will. . .

Please give me the strength and courage I need today.

THANK YOU, FATHER, FOR HEARING MY PRAYERS!

amen.

"Don't fear. Don't hesitate. Don't panic. God, your God, is right there with you, fighting with you against your enemies, fighting to win."
Deuteronomy 20:3–4 msg

DATE:

Dear Heavenly Father,

My gutsy prayer for today is. . .

I need You to. . .

With You by my side, I am unafraid because. . .

I believe You are the doer of the impossible because. . .

I know You will. . .

Please give me the strength and courage I need today.

THANK YOU, FATHER, FOR HEARING MY PRAYERS!

Amen.

Don't you know? Haven't you heard? The eternal God, the Lord, the Creator of the ends of the earth, doesn't grow tired or become weary. His understanding is beyond reach.

Isaiah 40:28–29 GW

DATE:

Dear Heavenly Father,

My gutsy prayer for today is. . .

I need You to. . .

With You by my side, I am unafraid because. . .

I believe You are the doer of the impossible because. . .

I know You will. . .

Please give me the strength and courage I need today.

THANK YOU, FATHER, FOR HEARING MY PRAYERS!

Amen.

The Scriptures impart to us encouragement and inspiration so that we can live in hope and endure all things.

ROMANS 15:4 TPT

DATE:

Dear Heavenly Father,

My gutsy prayer for today is. . .

I need You to. . .

With You by my side, I am unafraid because. . .

I believe You are the doer of the impossible because. . .

I know You will. . .

Please give me the strength and courage I need today.

THANK YOU, FATHER, FOR HEARING MY PRAYERS!

Amen.

God is my savior; I will trust him and not be afraid.
The L*ORD* *gives me power and strength; he is my savior.*
ISAIAH 12:2 GNT

DATE:

Dear Heavenly Father,

My gutsy prayer for today is. . .

I need You to. . .

With You by my side, I am unafraid because. . .

I believe You are the doer of the impossible because. . .

I know You will. . .

Please give me the strength and courage I need today.

THANK YOU, FATHER, FOR HEARING MY PRAYERS!

Amen.

He will keep you from every form of evil or calamity as he continuously watches over you. You will be guarded by God himself. You will be safe when you leave your home, and safely you will return. He will protect you now, and he'll protect you forevermore!

PSALM 121:7–8 TPT

DATE:

Dear Heavenly Father,

My gutsy prayer for today is. . .

I need You to. . .

With You by my side, I am unafraid because. . .

I believe You are the doer of the impossible because. . .

I know You will. . .

Please give me the strength and courage I need today.

THANK YOU, FATHER, FOR HEARING MY PRAYERS!

Amen.

Lord, so many times I fail; I fall into disgrace. But when I trust in you, I have a strong and glorious presence protecting and anointing me. Forever you're all I need!

PSALM 73:26 TPT

DATE:

Dear Heavenly Father,

My gutsy prayer for today is. . .

I need You to. . .

With You by my side, I am unafraid because. . .

I believe You are the doer of the impossible because. . .

I know You will. . .

Please give me the strength and courage I need today.

THANK YOU, FATHER, FOR HEARING MY PRAYERS!

Amen.

Let your hope keep you joyful, be patient in your troubles, and pray at all times.

ROMANS 12:12 GNT

DATE:

Dear Heavenly Father,

My gutsy prayer for today is. . .

I need You to. . .

With You by my side, I am unafraid because. . .

I believe You are the doer of the impossible because. . .

I know You will. . .

Please give me the strength and courage I need today.

THANK YOU, FATHER, FOR HEARING MY PRAYERS!

Amen.

"Truly, I tell you, if anyone says to this mountain, 'Go, throw yourself into the sea,' and does not doubt in their heart but believes that what they say will happen, it will be done for them."

MARK 11:23 NIV

DATE:

Dear Heavenly Father,

My gutsy prayer for today is. . .

I need You to. . .

With You by my side, I am unafraid because. . .

I believe You are the doer of the impossible because. . .

I know You will. . .

Please give me the strength and courage I need today.

THANK YOU, FATHER, FOR HEARING MY PRAYERS!

Amen.

Counting on God's Rule to prevail,
I take heart and gain strength. I run like a
deer. I feel like I'm king of the mountain!
Habakkuk 3:19 msg

DATE:

Dear Heavenly Father,

My gutsy prayer for today is. . .

I need You to. . .

With You by my side, I am unafraid because. . .

I believe You are the doer of the impossible because. . .

I know You will. . .

Please give me the strength and courage I need today.

THANK YOU, FATHER, FOR HEARING MY PRAYERS!

Amen.

Be brave. Be strong. Don't give up.
Expect God to get here soon.
PSALM 31:24 MSG

DATE:

Dear Heavenly Father,

My gutsy prayer for today is. . .

I need You to. . .

With You by my side, I am unafraid because. . .

I believe You are the doer of the impossible because. . .

I know You will. . .

Please give me the strength and courage I need today.

THANK YOU, FATHER, FOR HEARING MY PRAYERS!

Amen.

God is a safe place to hide, ready to help when we need him. We stand fearless at the cliff-edge of doom, courageous in seastorm and earthquake, before the rush and roar of oceans, the tremors that shift mountains.

PSALM 46:1–2 MSG

DATE:

Dear Heavenly Father,

My gutsy prayer for today is. . .

I need You to. . .

With You by my side, I am unafraid because. . .

I believe You are the doer of the impossible because. . .

I know You will. . .

Please give me the strength and courage I need today.

THANK YOU, FATHER, FOR HEARING MY PRAYERS!

Amen.

"In this godless world you will continue to experience difficulties. But take heart! I've conquered the world."

JOHN 16:33 MSG

DATE:

Dear Heavenly Father,

My gutsy prayer for today is. . .

I need You to. . .

With You by my side, I am unafraid because. . .

I believe You are the doer of the impossible because. . .

I know You will. . .

Please give me the strength and courage I need today.

THANK YOU, FATHER, FOR HEARING MY PRAYERS!

amen.

Jesus. . .addressed them: "I am the world's Light. No one who follows me stumbles around in the darkness. I provide plenty of light to live in."

John 8:12 MSG

DATE:

Dear Heavenly Father,

My gutsy prayer for today is. . .

I need You to. . .

With You by my side, I am unafraid because. . .

I believe You are the doer of the impossible because. . .

I know You will. . .

Please give me the strength and courage I need today.

THANK YOU, FATHER, FOR HEARING MY PRAYERS!

Amen.

Even when your path takes me through the valley of deepest darkness, fear will never conquer me, for you already have! . . . The comfort of your love takes away my fear. I'll never be lonely, for you are near.

Psalm 23:4 TPT

DATE:

Dear Heavenly Father,

My gutsy prayer for today is. . .

I need You to. . .

With You by my side, I am unafraid because. . .

I believe You are the doer of the impossible because. . .

I know You will. . .

Please give me the strength and courage I need today.

THANK YOU, FATHER, FOR HEARING MY PRAYERS!

Amen.

Pushed to the wall, I called to God; from the wide open spaces, he answered. God's now at my side and I'm not afraid; who would dare lay a hand on me?

Psalm 118:5–6 MSG

DATE:

Dear Heavenly Father,

My gutsy prayer for today is. . .

I need You to. . .

With You by my side, I am unafraid because. . .

I believe You are the doer of the impossible because. . .

I know You will. . .

Please give me the strength and courage I need today.

THANK YOU, FATHER, FOR HEARING MY PRAYERS!

Amen.

Lord, it is so much better to trust in you to save me than to put my confidence in someone else. Yes, it is so much better to trust in the Lord to save me than to put my confidence in celebrities.

Psalm 118:8–9 TPT

DATE:

Dear Heavenly Father,

My gutsy prayer for today is. . .

I need You to. . .

With You by my side, I am unafraid because. . .

I believe You are the doer of the impossible because. . .

I know You will. . .

Please give me the strength and courage I need today.

THANK YOU, FATHER, FOR HEARING MY PRAYERS!

amen.

They pushed hard to make me fall, but the Lord helped me. The Lord is my strength and my song. He is my savior.

Psalm 118:13–14 GW

DATE:

Dear Heavenly Father,

My gutsy prayer for today is. . .

I need You to. . .

With You by my side, I am unafraid because. . .

I believe You are the doer of the impossible because. . .

I know You will. . .

Please give me the strength and courage I need today.

THANK YOU, FATHER, FOR HEARING MY PRAYERS!

amen.

The Lord protects and defends me;
I trust in him. He gives me help and makes
me glad; I praise him with joyful songs.

Psalm 28:7 GNT

DATE:

Dear Heavenly Father,

My gutsy prayer for today is. . .

I need You to. . .

With You by my side, I am unafraid because. . .

I believe You are the doer of the impossible because. . .

I know You will. . .

Please give me the strength and courage I need today.

THANK YOU, FATHER, FOR HEARING MY PRAYERS!

amen.

Steep your life in God-reality, God-initiative,
God-provisions. Don't worry about missing out.
You'll find all your everyday human concerns will be met.

Matthew 6:33 msg

DATE:

Dear Heavenly Father,

My gutsy prayer for today is. . .

I need You to. . .

With You by my side, I am unafraid because. . .

I believe You are the doer of the impossible because. . .

I know You will. . .

Please give me the strength and courage I need today.

THANK YOU, FATHER, FOR HEARING MY PRAYERS!

Amen.

I love you, Yahweh, and I'm bonded to you,
my strength! Yahweh, you're the bedrock beneath
my feet, my faith-fortress, my wonderful deliverer. . . .
You're the shield around me, the mighty power
that saves me, and my high place.

PSALM 18:1–2 TPT

DATE:

Dear Heavenly Father,

My gutsy prayer for today is. . .

I need You to. . .

With You by my side, I am unafraid because. . .

I believe You are the doer of the impossible because. . .

I know You will. . .

Please give me the strength and courage I need today.

THANK YOU, FATHER, FOR HEARING MY PRAYERS!

Amen.

I'm asking God to give you a gift from the wealth of his glory. I pray that he would give you inner strength and power through his Spirit.

Ephesians 3:16 GW

DATE:

Dear Heavenly Father,

My gutsy prayer for today is. . .

I need You to. . .

With You by my side, I am unafraid because. . .

I believe You are the doer of the impossible because. . .

I know You will. . .

Please give me the strength and courage I need today.

THANK YOU, FATHER, FOR HEARING MY PRAYERS!

Amen.

The LORD *your God is with you. He is a hero who saves you. He happily rejoices over you, renews you with his love, and celebrates over you with shouts of joy.*

ZEPHANIAH 3:17 GW

DATE:

Dear Heavenly Father,

My gutsy prayer for today is. . .

I need You to. . .

With You by my side, I am unafraid because. . .

I believe You are the doer of the impossible because. . .

I know You will. . .

Please give me the strength and courage I need today.

THANK YOU, FATHER, FOR HEARING MY PRAYERS!

amen.

I'm sure now I'll see God's goodness in the exuberant earth. Stay with God! Take heart. Don't quit. I'll say it again: Stay with God.

Psalm 27:13–14 msg

DATE:

Dear Heavenly Father,

My gutsy prayer for today is. . .

I need You to. . .

With You by my side, I am unafraid because. . .

I believe You are the doer of the impossible because. . .

I know You will. . .

Please give me the strength and courage I need today.

THANK YOU, FATHER, FOR HEARING MY PRAYERS!

Amen.

"I leave the gift of peace with you—my peace. Not the kind of fragile peace given by the world, but my perfect peace. Don't yield to fear or be troubled in your hearts—instead, be courageous!"

JOHN 14:27 TPT

DATE:

Dear Heavenly Father,

My gutsy prayer for today is. . .

I need You to. . .

With You by my side, I am unafraid because. . .

I believe You are the doer of the impossible because. . .

I know You will. . .

Please give me the strength and courage I need today.

THANK YOU, FATHER, FOR HEARING MY PRAYERS!

Amen.

Thank you for your love, thank you for your faithfulness; most holy is your name, most holy is your Word. The moment I called out, you stepped in; you made my life large with strength.

PSALM 138:2–3 MSG

DATE:

Dear Heavenly Father,

My gutsy prayer for today is. . .

I need You to. . .

With You by my side, I am unafraid because. . .

I believe You are the doer of the impossible because. . .

I know You will. . .

Please give me the strength and courage I need today.

THANK YOU, FATHER, FOR HEARING MY PRAYERS!

Amen.

God means what he says. What he says goes. . . .
Nothing and no one can resist God's Word.
We can't get away from it—no matter what.
HEBREWS 4:12–13 MSG

DATE:

Dear Heavenly Father,

My gutsy prayer for today is. . .

I need You to. . .

With You by my side, I am unafraid because. . .

I believe You are the doer of the impossible because. . .

I know You will. . .

Please give me the strength and courage I need today.

THANK YOU, FATHER, FOR HEARING MY PRAYERS!

Amen.

He is the God who makes me strong, who makes my pathway safe. He makes me sure-footed as a deer; he keeps me safe on the mountains. He trains me for battle, so that I can use the strongest bow.

Psalm 18:32–34 GNT

DATE:

Dear Heavenly Father,

My gutsy prayer for today is. . .

I need You to. . .

With You by my side, I am unafraid because. . .

I believe You are the doer of the impossible because. . .

I know You will. . .

Please give me the strength and courage I need today.

THANK YOU, FATHER, FOR HEARING MY PRAYERS!

amen.

The Holy Spirit takes hold of us in our human frailty to empower us in our weakness. For example, at times we don't even know how to pray, or know the best things to ask for. But the Holy Spirit rises up within us to super-intercede on our behalf.

ROMANS 8:26 TPT

DATE:

Dear Heavenly Father,

My gutsy prayer for today is. . .

I need You to. . .

With You by my side, I am unafraid because. . .

I believe You are the doer of the impossible because. . .

I know You will. . .

Please give me the strength and courage I need today.

THANK YOU, FATHER, FOR HEARING MY PRAYERS!

amen.

So be content with who you are, and don't put on airs. God's strong hand is on you; he'll promote you at the right time. Live carefree before God; he is most careful with you.

1 Peter 5:6–7 msg

DATE:

Dear Heavenly Father,

My gutsy prayer for today is. . .

I need You to. . .

With You by my side, I am unafraid because. . .

I believe You are the doer of the impossible because. . .

I know You will. . .

Please give me the strength and courage I need today.

THANK YOU, FATHER, FOR HEARING MY PRAYERS!

amen.

"Don't be afraid. You are highly respected. Everything is alright! Be strong! Be strong!"

DANIEL 10:19 GW

DATE:

Dear Heavenly Father,

My gutsy prayer for today is. . .

I need You to. . .

With You by my side, I am unafraid because. . .

I believe You are the doer of the impossible because. . .

I know You will. . .

Please give me the strength and courage I need today.

THANK YOU, FATHER, FOR HEARING MY PRAYERS!

Amen.

People cannot save themselves.
But with God, all things are possible.
MATTHEW 19:26 VOICE

DATE:

Dear Heavenly Father,

My gutsy prayer for today is. . .

I need You to. . .

With You by my side, I am unafraid because. . .

I believe You are the doer of the impossible because. . .

I know You will. . .

Please give me the strength and courage I need today.

THANK YOU, FATHER, FOR HEARING MY PRAYERS!

amen.

Never doubt God's mighty power. . . . He will achieve infinitely more than your greatest request, your most unbelievable dream, and exceed your wildest imagination!

EPHESIANS 3:20 TPT

DATE:

Dear Heavenly Father,

My gutsy prayer for today is. . .

I need You to. . .

With You by my side, I am unafraid because. . .

I believe You are the doer of the impossible because. . .

I know You will. . .

Please give me the strength and courage I need today.

THANK YOU, FATHER, FOR HEARING MY PRAYERS!

amen.

"Eternal Lord, with Your outstretched arm and Your enormous power You created the heavens and the earth. Nothing is too difficult for You."

JEREMIAH 32:17 VOICE

DATE:

Dear Heavenly Father,

My gutsy prayer for today is. . .

I need You to. . .

With You by my side, I am unafraid because. . .

I believe You are the doer of the impossible because. . .

I know You will. . .

Please give me the strength and courage I need today.

THANK YOU, FATHER, FOR HEARING MY PRAYERS!

amen.

And then, after your brief suffering, the God of all loving grace, who has called you to share in his eternal glory in Christ, will personally and powerfully restore you and make you stronger than ever.

1 Peter 5:10 TPT

DATE:

Dear Heavenly Father,

My gutsy prayer for today is. . .

I need You to. . .

With You by my side, I am unafraid because. . .

I believe You are the doer of the impossible because. . .

I know You will. . .

Please give me the strength and courage I need today.

THANK YOU, FATHER, FOR HEARING MY PRAYERS!

amen.

We can't round up enough containers to hold everything God generously pours into our lives through the Holy Spirit!

Romans 5:5 MSG

DATE:

Dear Heavenly Father,

My gutsy prayer for today is. . .

I need You to. . .

With You by my side, I am unafraid because. . .

I believe You are the doer of the impossible because. . .

I know You will. . .

Please give me the strength and courage I need today.

THANK YOU, FATHER, FOR HEARING MY PRAYERS!

Amen.

Lord, . . .I cling to your commands and follow them as closely as I can. I will run after you with delight in my heart, for you will make me obedient to your instructions.

PSALM 119:31–32 TPT

DATE:

Dear Heavenly Father,

My gutsy prayer for today is. . .

I need You to. . .

With You by my side, I am unafraid because. . .

I believe You are the doer of the impossible because. . .

I know You will. . .

Please give me the strength and courage I need today.

THANK YOU, FATHER, FOR HEARING MY PRAYERS!

Amen.

Do not forget Your promise to Your servant; through it You have given me hope. This brings me solace in the midst of my troubles: that Your word has revived me.

PSALM 119:49–50 VOICE

DATE:

Dear Heavenly Father,

My gutsy prayer for today is. . .

I need You to. . .

With You by my side, I am unafraid because. . .

I believe You are the doer of the impossible because. . .

I know You will. . .

Please give me the strength and courage I need today.

THANK YOU, FATHER, FOR HEARING MY PRAYERS!

amen.

But I will sing about your strength. In the morning I will joyfully sing about your mercy. You have been my stronghold and a place of safety in times of trouble.

PSALM 59:16 GW

DATE:

Dear Heavenly Father,

My gutsy prayer for today is. . .

I need You to. . .

With You by my side, I am unafraid because. . .

I will watch for You, for You keep me strong.
God, You are my security! My God is one step
ahead of me with His mercy; He will show
me the victory I desire over my enemies.

PSALM 59:9–10 VOICE

DATE:

Dear Heavenly Father,

My gutsy prayer for today is. . .

I need You to. . .

With You by my side, I am unafraid because. . .

I believe You are the doer of the impossible because...

I know You will...

Please give me the strength and courage I need today.

THANK YOU, FATHER, FOR HEARING MY PRAYERS!

amen.

Here's what I've learned through it all: Don't give up; don't be impatient; be entwined as one with the Lord. Be brave and courageous, and never lose hope. Yes, keep on waiting—for he will never disappoint you!

PSALM 27:14 TPT

DATE:

Dear Heavenly Father,

My gutsy prayer for today is. . .

I need You to. . .

With You by my side, I am unafraid because. . .

I believe You are the doer of the impossible because. . .

I know You will. . .

Please give me the strength and courage I need today.

THANK YOU, FATHER, FOR HEARING MY PRAYERS!

Amen.

Honest people are relaxed and confident, bold as lions.

PROVERBS 28:1 MSG

DATE:

Dear Heavenly Father,

My gutsy prayer for today is. . .

I need You to. . .

With You by my side, I am unafraid because. . .

I believe You are the doer of the impossible because...

I know You will...

Please give me the strength and courage I need today.

THANK YOU, FATHER, FOR HEARING MY PRAYERS!

Amen.

Now my beloved ones, I have saved these most important truths for last: Be supernaturally infused with strength through your life-union with the Lord Jesus. Stand victorious with the force of his explosive power flowing in and through you.

EPHESIANS 6:10 TPT

DATE:

Dear Heavenly Father,

My gutsy prayer for today is. . .

I need You to. . .

With You by my side, I am unafraid because. . .

I believe You are the doer of the impossible because. . .

I know You will. . .

Please give me the strength and courage I need today.

THANK YOU, FATHER, FOR HEARING MY PRAYERS!

amen.

"Now, remember, it is I who sends you out, even though you feel vulnerable as lambs going into a pack of wolves. So be as shrewd as snakes yet as harmless as doves."

MATTHEW 10:16 TPT

DATE:

Dear Heavenly Father,

My gutsy prayer for today is. . .

I need You to. . .

With You by my side, I am unafraid because. . .

I believe You are the doer of the impossible because. . .

I know You will. . .

Please give me the strength and courage I need today.

THANK YOU, FATHER, FOR HEARING MY PRAYERS!

Amen.

The wise counsel GOD *gives when I'm awake is confirmed by my sleeping heart. Day and night I'll stick with* GOD*; I've got a good thing going and I'm not letting go.*

PSALM 16:7–8 MSG

DATE:

Dear Heavenly Father,

My gutsy prayer for today is. . .

I need You to. . .

With You by my side, I am unafraid because. . .

I believe You are the doer of the impossible because. . .

I know You will. . .

Please give me the strength and courage I need today.

THANK YOU, FATHER, FOR HEARING MY PRAYERS!

Amen.

I lay all my fears before you and trust in you with all my heart. What harm could a man bring to me? With God on my side, I will not be afraid of what comes. The roaring praises of God fill my heart as I trust his promises.

PSALM 56:3–4 TPT

DATE:

Dear Heavenly Father,

My gutsy prayer for today is. . .

I need You to. . .

With You by my side, I am unafraid because. . .

I believe You are the doer of the impossible because. . .

I know You will. . .

Please give me the strength and courage I need today.

THANK YOU, FATHER, FOR HEARING MY PRAYERS!

Amen.

What will separate us from the love Christ has for us? Can trouble, distress, persecution, hunger, nakedness, danger, or violent death separate us from his love?

ROMANS 8:35 GW

DATE:

Dear Heavenly Father,

My gutsy prayer for today is. . .

I need You to. . .

With You by my side, I am unafraid because. . .

I believe You are the doer of the impossible because. . .

I know You will. . .

Please give me the strength and courage I need today.

THANK YOU, FATHER, FOR HEARING MY PRAYERS!

Amen.

"Remember that I am always with you until the end of time."
MATTHEW 28:20 GW

DATE:

Dear Heavenly Father,

My gutsy prayer for today is. . .

I need You to. . .

With You by my side, I am unafraid because. . .

I believe You are the doer of the impossible because. . .

I know You will. . .

Please give me the strength and courage I need today.

THANK YOU, FATHER, FOR HEARING MY PRAYERS!

Amen.

My dear brothers and sisters, stay firmly planted—be unshakable—do many good works in the name of God, and know that all your labor is not for nothing when it is for God.

1 CORINTHIANS 15:58 VOICE

DATE:

Dear Heavenly Father,

My gutsy prayer for today is. . .

I need You to. . .

With You by my side, I am unafraid because. . .

I believe You are the doer of the impossible because...

I know You will...

Please give me the strength and courage I need today.

THANK YOU, FATHER, FOR HEARING MY PRAYERS!

Amen.

So we can say with great confidence:
"I know the Lord is for me and I will never be afraid of what people may do to me!"
HEBREWS 13:6 TPT

DATE:

Dear Heavenly Father,

My gutsy prayer for today is. . .

I need You to. . .

With You by my side, I am unafraid because. . .

I believe You are the doer of the impossible because...

I know You will...

Please give me the strength and courage I need today.

THANK YOU, FATHER, FOR HEARING MY PRAYERS!

Amen.

Reach down from your heavens and rescue me from this hell and deliver me from these dark powers. They speak nothing but lies; their words are pure deceit. Nothing they say can ever be trusted.

PSALM 144:7–8 TPT

DATE:

Dear Heavenly Father,

My gutsy prayer for today is. . .

I need You to. . .

With You by my side, I am unafraid because. . .

I believe You are the doer of the impossible because. . .

I know You will. . .

Please give me the strength and courage I need today.

THANK YOU, FATHER, FOR HEARING MY PRAYERS!

Amen.

Entrust your ways to the Lord.
Trust him, and he will act on your behalf.
Psalm 37:5 GW

DATE:

Dear Heavenly Father,

My gutsy prayer for today is. . .

I need You to. . .

With You by my side, I am unafraid because. . .

I believe You are the doer of the impossible because...

I know You will...

Please give me the strength and courage I need today.

THANK YOU, FATHER, FOR HEARING MY PRAYERS!

amen.

Thank God that he gives us the victory through our Lord Jesus Christ.

1 CORINTHIANS 15:57 GW

DATE:

Dear Heavenly Father,

My gutsy prayer for today is. . .

I need You to. . .

With You by my side, I am unafraid because. . .

I believe You are the doer of the impossible because. . .

I know You will. . .

Please give me the strength and courage I need today.

THANK YOU, FATHER, FOR HEARING MY PRAYERS!

Amen.

With his breath he scatters the schemes of
nations who oppose him; they will never succeed.
His destiny-plan for the earth stands sure.
His forever-plan remains in place and will never fail.

PSALM 33:10–11 TPT

DATE:

Dear Heavenly Father,

My gutsy prayer for today is. . .

I need You to. . .

With You by my side, I am unafraid because. . .

I believe You are the doer of the impossible because. . .

I know You will. . .

Please give me the strength and courage I need today.

THANK YOU, FATHER, FOR HEARING MY PRAYERS!

Amen.

Watch this: God's eye is on those who respect him, the ones who are looking for his love. He's ready to come to their rescue in bad times; in lean times he keeps body and soul together.

PSALM 33:18–19 MSG

DATE:

Dear Heavenly Father,

My gutsy prayer for today is. . .

I need You to. . .

With You by my side, I am unafraid because. . .

I believe You are the doer of the impossible because. . .

I know You will. . .

Please give me the strength and courage I need today.

THANK YOU, FATHER, FOR HEARING MY PRAYERS!

amen.

We're depending on God; he's everything we need.
What's more, our hearts brim with joy since we've
taken for our own his holy name. Love us, God,
with all you've got—that's what we're depending on.

Psalm 33:20–22 MSG

DATE:

Dear Heavenly Father,

My gutsy prayer for today is. . .

I need You to. . .

With You by my side, I am unafraid because. . .

I believe You are the doer of the impossible because. . .

I know You will. . .

Please give me the strength and courage I need today.

THANK YOU, FATHER, FOR HEARING MY PRAYERS!

Amen.

God, my shepherd! I don't need a thing. You have bedded me down in lush meadows, you find me quiet pools to drink from. True to your word, you let me catch my breath and send me in the right direction.

Psalm 23:1–3 MSG

DATE:

Dear Heavenly Father,

My gutsy prayer for today is. . .

I need You to. . .

With You by my side, I am unafraid because. . .

I believe You are the doer of the impossible because. . .

I know You will. . .

Please give me the strength and courage I need today.

THANK YOU, FATHER, FOR HEARING MY PRAYERS!

Amen.

I know that your goodness and love will be with me all my life; and your house will be my home as long as I live.

PSALM 23:6 GNT

DATE:

Dear Heavenly Father,

My gutsy prayer for today is. . .

I need You to. . .

With You by my side, I am unafraid because. . .

I believe You are the doer of the impossible because. . .

I know You will. . .

Please give me the strength and courage I need today.

THANK YOU, FATHER, FOR HEARING MY PRAYERS!

Amen.

God stuck by me. He stood me up on a wide-open field; I stood there saved—surprised to be loved!

Psalm 18:18 MSG

DATE:

Dear Heavenly Father,

My gutsy prayer for today is. . .

I need You to. . .

With You by my side, I am unafraid because. . .

I believe You are the doer of the impossible because. . .

I know You will. . .

Please give me the strength and courage I need today.

THANK YOU, FATHER, FOR HEARING MY PRAYERS!

Amen.

God, all at once you turned on a floodlight for me! You are the revelation-light in my darkness, and in your brightness I can see the path ahead.

PSALM 18:28 TPT

DATE:

Dear Heavenly Father,

My gutsy prayer for today is. . .

I need You to. . .

With You by my side, I am unafraid because. . .

I believe You are the doer of the impossible because. . .

I know You will. . .

Please give me the strength and courage I need today.

THANK YOU, FATHER, FOR HEARING MY PRAYERS!

Amen.

You empower me for victory with your wraparound presence. Your power within makes me strong to subdue. By stooping down in gentleness, you made me great! You've set me free, and now I'm standing complete!

PSALM 18:35–36 TPT

DATE:

Dear Heavenly Father,

My gutsy prayer for today is. . .

I need You to. . .

With You by my side, I am unafraid because. . .

I believe You are the doer of the impossible because. . .

I know You will. . .

Please give me the strength and courage I need today.

THANK YOU, FATHER, FOR HEARING MY PRAYERS!

Amen.

"But I have kept you in power for a reason, to show you My greater power and to see that My name and reputation spread through all the earth."

EXODUS 9:16 VOICE

DATE:

Dear Heavenly Father,

My gutsy prayer for today is. . .

I need You to. . .

With You by my side, I am unafraid because. . .

I believe You are the doer of the impossible because. . .

I know You will. . .

Please give me the strength and courage I need today.

THANK YOU, FATHER, FOR HEARING MY PRAYERS!

Amen.

"Yes. I'll stay with you, I'll protect you wherever you go, and I'll bring you back to this very ground. I'll stick with you until I've done everything I promised you."

GENESIS 28:15 MSG

DATE:

Dear Heavenly Father,

My gutsy prayer for today is. . .

I need You to. . .

With You by my side, I am unafraid because. . .

My delightfully loved friends, when our hearts don't condemn us, we have a bold freedom to speak face-to-face with God.

1 John 3:21 TPT

DATE:

Dear Heavenly Father,

My gutsy prayer for today is. . .

I need You to. . .

With You by my side, I am unafraid because. . .

I believe You are the doer of the impossible because. . .

I know You will. . .

Please give me the strength and courage I need today.

THANK YOU, FATHER, FOR HEARING MY PRAYERS!

Amen.

We live in the bold confidence that God hears our voices when we ask for things that fit His plan. And if we have no doubt that He hears our voices, we can be assured that He moves in response to our call.

1 John 5:14–15 VOICE

DATE:

Dear Heavenly Father,

My gutsy prayer for today is. . .

I need You to. . .

With You by my side, I am unafraid because. . .

I believe You are the doer of the impossible because. . .

I know You will. . .

Please give me the strength and courage I need today.

THANK YOU, FATHER, FOR HEARING MY PRAYERS!

amen.

"I am Yahweh*, your mighty God! I grip your right hand and won't let you go! I whisper to you: 'Don't be afraid; I am here to help you!' "*

Isaiah 41:13 TPT

DATE:

Dear Heavenly Father,

My gutsy prayer for today is. . .

I need You to. . .

With You by my side, I am unafraid because. . .

I believe You are the doer of the impossible because. . .

I know You will. . .

Please give me the strength and courage I need today.

THANK YOU, FATHER, FOR HEARING MY PRAYERS!

Amen.

I love the Lord, *because he hears me; he listens to*
my prayers. He listens to me every time I call to him.
The danger of death was all around me; the horrors of the
grave closed in on me; I was filled with fear and anxiety.
Then I called to the Lord, *"I beg you,* Lord, *save me!"*
Psalm 116:1–4 GNT

DATE:

Dear Heavenly Father,

My gutsy prayer for today is. . .

I need You to. . .

With You by my side, I am unafraid because. . .

I believe You are the doer of the impossible because. . .

I know You will. . .

Please give me the strength and courage I need today.

THANK YOU, FATHER, FOR HEARING MY PRAYERS!

Amen.

The Lord is merciful and good; our God is compassionate. The Lord protects the helpless; when I was in danger, he saved me. Be confident, my heart, because the Lord has been good to me.

Psalm 116:5–7 GNT

DATE:

Dear Heavenly Father,

My gutsy prayer for today is. . .

I need You to. . .

With You by my side, I am unafraid because. . .

I believe You are the doer of the impossible because. . .

I know You will. . .

Please give me the strength and courage I need today.

THANK YOU, FATHER, FOR HEARING MY PRAYERS!

Amen.

And my Lord will continue to deliver me from every form of evil and give me life in his heavenly kingdom. May all the glory go to him alone for all the ages of eternity!

2 TIMOTHY 4:18 TPT

DATE:

Dear Heavenly Father,

My gutsy prayer for today is. . .

I need You to. . .

With You by my side, I am unafraid because. . .

When you pray, you must believe and not doubt at all. Whoever doubts is like a wave in the sea that is driven and blown about by the wind.

James 1:6 GNT

DATE:

Dear Heavenly Father,

My gutsy prayer for today is. . .

I need You to. . .

With You by my side, I am unafraid because. . .

Anyone who meets a testing challenge head-on and manages to stick it out is mighty fortunate. For such persons loyally in love with God, the reward is life and more life.

James 1:12 MSG

DATE:

Dear Heavenly Father,

My gutsy prayer for today is. . .

I need You to. . .

With You by my side, I am unafraid because. . .

I believe You are the doer of the impossible because. . .

I know You will. . .

Please give me the strength and courage I need today.

THANK YOU, FATHER, FOR HEARING MY PRAYERS!

Amen.

Now you've got my feet on the life path,
all radiant from the shining of your face.
Ever since you took my hand, I'm on the right way.

PSALM 16:11 MSG

DATE:

Dear Heavenly Father,

My gutsy prayer for today is. . .

I need You to. . .

With You by my side, I am unafraid because. . .

I believe You are the doer of the impossible because. . .

I know You will. . .

Please give me the strength and courage I need today.

THANK YOU, FATHER, FOR HEARING MY PRAYERS!

amen.

A joyful, cheerful heart brings healing to both body and soul.

PROVERBS 17:22 TPT

DATE:

Dear Heavenly Father,

My gutsy prayer for today is. . .

I need You to. . .

With You by my side, I am unafraid because. . .

I believe You are the doer of the impossible because. . .

I know You will. . .

Please give me the strength and courage I need today.

THANK YOU, FATHER, FOR HEARING MY PRAYERS!

Amen.

All you saints! Sing your hearts out to God!
Thank him to his face! He gets angry once in a while,
but across a lifetime there is only love. The nights of
crying your eyes out give way to days of laughter.

Psalm 30:4–5 MSG

DATE:

Dear Heavenly Father,

My gutsy prayer for today is. . .

I need You to. . .

With You by my side, I am unafraid because. . .

I believe You are the doer of the impossible because. . .

I know You will. . .

Please give me the strength and courage I need today.

THANK YOU, FATHER, FOR HEARING MY PRAYERS!

amen.

This is the day the Eternal God has made;
let us celebrate and be happy today.
PSALM 118:24 VOICE

Discover More Faith Maps for the Entire Family

The Prayer Map for Men
978-1-64352-438-2

The Prayer Map for Women
978-1-63609-763-3

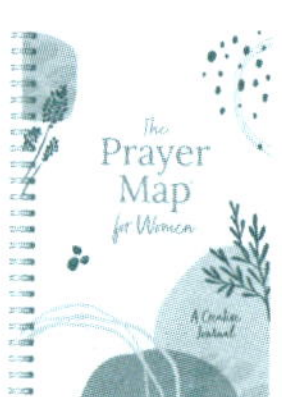

The Prayer Map for Women
978-1-63609-762-6

The Prayer Map for Teen Girls
978-1-63609-803-6

The Prayer Map for Girls
978-1-68322-559-1

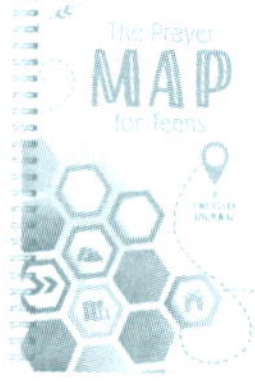

The Prayer Map for Teens
978-1-68322-556-0

The Prayer Map for Boys
978-1-68322-558-4

These purposeful prayer journals are a fun and creative way to fully experience the power of prayer. Each page guides you to write out thoughts, ideas, and lists. . .creating a specific "map" for you to follow as you talk to God. Each map includes a spot to record the date so you can look back on your prayers and see how God has worked in your life. *The Prayer Map* will not only encourage you to spend time talking with God about the things that matter most. . .it will also help you build a healthy spiritual habit of continual prayer for life!

Spiral Bound